What I Believe

Matthew Robert Payne

Dedication

I want to dedicate this book to my mother. My mother has seen me healthy, and she has seen me ill and deceived. Through it all, through all the years of deception, she was kind, full of faith, and full of love. She is my delight, my closest friend, and my best supporter.

I want to also give a shout out to Mary Gibson, who is also a great friend and supporter. I call my mother every day and call Mary nearly every day as well. There is nothing like having women in your life to love and support you in all that you do.

Acknowledgements

I want to thank my mother and father for all the love that they have given me. I want to thank Jesus, the Father, and the Holy Spirit for being part of my life and for leading me. I want to thank all of my friends who love and support me. I want to thank Bill Vincent from Revival Waves of Glory Books & Publishing for publishing my books and Lisa Thompson for editing so many of my books. You can contact her at writebylisa@gmail.com for your editing needs. I also want to thank the people who have sown into my ministry who made it possible for me to publish this book. I feel that this is an important book so that people understand the fundamental principles that I believe.

I want to thank you, the reader, for deciding to buy this book and for believing in me enough to read it. I hope that you have been blessed by some of my books already. If this is the first book of mine that you have read, I hope that this book will encourage you to read more of my books.

Table of Contents

Introduction

I was reading the book, _40 Days in Heaven_, where the main character met with a number of saints, including Moses, Paul, Abraham, and Peter, when they were discussing theology. He asked them for a statement of their beliefs and therefore of the truth that they held to. Later during the trip in heaven, these elders gave the character a scroll with a statement of beliefs. In the following pages, I quote the twenty-one points in that scroll. I will then add some of my own points to that list in a separate section.

I agree with all these points with only one exception: I have seen God myself in visions in heaven. I thought it would be helpful for my readers to have an idea of what I personally believe since I write so many books and am considered a teacher and prophet by God.

I will endeavor to put these on my website so that people can easily find them. I have been led by the Holy Spirit to make this into a book, and I encourage you all to buy the book, _40 Days in Heaven_, from which they came.

The Theology of the Elders

This is the adapted content of the elders' scroll as found in the book, *40 Days in Heaven*.

1. There is but one living and true God.

His Attributes
2. The attributes of God are the qualities, elements, and perfections that belong to him. They are parts of his divine nature—not that his whole being consists of a combination of them but because they are the forms and expressions of his being that he has revealed to man.

3. These attributes are natural and moral. The natural attributes reveal his existence as an infinite and rational spirit that is self-existent and that operates in freedom, omnipotence, omnipresence, omniscience, and wisdom.

The moral attributes are holiness, righteousness, justice, goodness, love, grace, mercy, and truth.

4. God is an invisible Spirit, whom no man has seen nor can see as known to men on earth. He is eternal and self-existent. He creates immortal beings, but God alone possesses eternity. He is infinite, filling all space in the entire universe, embracing all worlds. He is omnipresent, or infinite in power, shown by all his creations from the infinitely great to the infinitely small. All his acts are done by the exercise of his volition and are seen by man

in the universality, variety, and multitude of his works. God's omnipotence is limited only by his moral perfections. God cannot lie nor do any bad act although he has the power.

5. God is omnipresent, the Creator, Upholder, and Governor of all things. He is also omniscient, and all things are open and naked before his eyes. God's wisdom is infinite, embracing all knowledge, and is independent of all his creatures. We can tell him nothing that he does not know, but his intelligent, infinite intuition comprehends all things: past, present, or future. This intelligence is perfect and absolute. Man analyzes things to find out their nature. God knows the nature without the analysis.

6. The foreknowledge of God is also absolute. How the foreknowledge of God is to be reconciled with man's free agency and moral accountability is indeed to men in the world a dark problem, but, in the scriptures, both are clearly taught, and faith accepts what reason cannot reconcile. Some churches have denied man's moral freedom. Others maintain that God, in the exercise of his omniscience, like his omnipotence, abstains from knowing what his creatures will do under certain given circumstances. But the foreknowledge of God itself, unrevealed to men, does not impose nor even hint at any course of behavior whatsoever; it in no degree affects his liberty of action. Man neither sins nor follows holiness as the result of God's foreknowledge; so notwithstanding God's foreknowledge, he has made man in his image, a free moral being.

7. God is infinitely wise, always knows what is best, and always adopts means that will best accomplish his purposes. That is wisdom, for wisdom is the art of turning our knowledge to the best account. God's wisdom is seen in both creation and providence. His wisdom and his works everywhere confirm each other as being of God. No higher wisdom has ever been seen or known than God's wisdom in the plan of human redemption. This solves the problem of God's justice in justifying the believer in Jesus Christ.

8. The perfect goodness of God is seen in the benevolence that embraces all mankind and provides for their welfare. His merciful dealings with men declare his goodness. It is also seen in his unmerited favor, drawing man to salvation, and in the use of so many means to this end as well as in the abundant provision that he has made for man's present and eternal happiness.

Moral Evil
9. How sin can exist in the world with all its terrible consequences in connection with God's righteous government is an awful and difficult problem, and man cannot possibly reconcile the complete solution of this in his earthly life. But sin does exist, and God permits it for reasons of his own not fully revealed to men. In heaven, it could not be so. No taint of sin can ever enter the gates of this city. If an angel should again sin, God would instantly cast him down to hell.

10. Righteousness and justice are divine perfections, holiness exhibited in government. Truth or faithfulness of

God is much the same as his righteousness. All he says and does is true. His truthfulness is an element of his character. God cannot lie. As God is eternal, his truth remains the same. Whatever is out of harmony with his revealed truth is a lie. The question, "What is truth?" has the following answer that we repeat in heaven: "To know God as he has revealed himself to man is truth of the highest order." Our Lord declared, "I am the way, the truth, and the life." (See John 14:6.) All things taught or believed that are out of harmony with his clear revelations are both false and misleading.

The Triune God

11. The eternal God has revealed himself to men as Father, Son, and Holy Ghost. The Son of God is and always was divine. He is the express image of the Father. The church has embraced many errors and heresies in past ages. But we worship one Triune God, neither confounding the persons nor dividing the substances of them. For there is one person of the Father, another of the Son, and another of the Holy Ghost—but the Godhead of the Father, Son, and Holy Ghost is one God.

The Divinity of Jesus Christ

12. He was the Word of God from eternity. In the beginning was the Word, and the Word was with God, and the Word was God. (See John 1:1.) While on earth, we always held him to be divine and worshipped him as God, and, in heaven, he is confessed by all, both saints and angels, to be God and equal to the Father. All the hosts of heaven worship him. He was God manifest in the flesh.

The Holy Spirit

13. The Holy Ghost is one with the Father and with the Son—equal in eternity, power, and glory. In creation, he moved upon the face of the waters and developed form and beauty out of disorder and confusion. He proceeded from the Father and from the Son and took up his abode with his church on earth. He has been with them ever since his coming at Pentecost. He is the comforter, guide, and sanctifier of his people.

Man's Original State and Fall

14. God made man upright. He was both material and spiritual and possessed of a divine life and made in the image of God. He could hold communion with God with all that is divine and with the material universe. He was made but a little lower than the angels and was crowned with glory and honor and had dominion over the works of God's hands in the earth. He was a companion of his Father and Creator, capable of admiring, adoring, and enjoying God. He was material and possessed an animal nature. Yet he came from the hands of God and was an intellectual, moral, pure, and holy being. He was placed under law with life and death before him. Adam rebelled; sin was born on earth. The glory of the Lord departed from him. Man fell and felt his guilt and was alienated from God. The stream of humanity was contaminated at its source. The first pair became sinful. Their descendants of necessity were fallen and depraved in their image. So by one man sin and then death entered into the world, and so death passed upon all men, for all have sinned. Our nature sinned in Adam, and the stream became polluted at the fountain head. This depravity became

universal, for all the faculties and powers of the soul and body were brought under the power of evil.

The Atonement

15. We universally believe that the death of Christ was vicarious and propitiatory and that by it divine justice is satisfied. God can be just and the justifier of all who believe in Christ Jesus, and that pardon and salvation is freely offered to all men upon repentance and faith. All men throughout the ages who would accept and be willing to conform to this plan should be saved so that everyone in harmony with his power and liberty of choice who shall choose eternal life though God's plan was foreordained to eternal salvation.

Election and Foreordination

16. We believe God did foreordain and devise a plan from the foundation of the world by which he would save man, and further, he did foreordain from the beginning that all men throughout the ages who would accept and be willing to conform to this plan should be saved so that everyone in harmony with his power and liberty of choice who shall choose eternal life though God's plan was foreordained to eternal salvation.

Repentance

17. True repentance is a condition of the soul before God brought about by the operations of the Spirit of God upon the heart and soul of man whereby he is made to see and feel the sinfulness of his sins and also to forsake them utterly and with full purpose of heart to yield obedience to God in the future.

Justification

18. Justification can only follow true repentance and is an act of God's free grace wherein he pardons the sins of man and accepts him as righteous in his sight only for the sake of Christ.

Faith

19. True unfeigned faith in God believes all that God has said, commanded, promised, or threatened. It is dependent upon testimony and is valuable to us as the truth itself. We can believe in men. We are responsible for our faith, for one might believe a lie as he does the truth. The truth only can make him free. True saving faith leads the soul to trust itself to the all-atoning merits of the sacrificial death and resurrection of Jesus Christ.

Adoption

20. Adoption is an act of God whereby the believing sinner is received into the family of God with all the rights and privileges of his children in which he becomes an heir of God with a right and title to eternal life.

The New Birth

21. The new birth of which our Lord spoke (see John 3) is that mighty change made by God in the soul of man when God imparts to him eternal life and renews him in the image of God. This change is the work of the Holy Spirit brought about in man, convincing him of sin, and leading him to repentance and faith whereby he is born from above with eternal life as a gift from God.

Additional Beliefs I Hold

Saints

I personally believe in the verse found in John 14:21 where Jesus said that it would be possible for us to do greater works on earth than he did. Jesus met with Elijah and Moses on the Mount of Transfiguration, and they comforted him and gave him strength to face the cross. I believe that people who know Jesus on earth and who have a relationship with the Holy Spirit can be visited by saints from heaven today, people who have passed on before us. I have met many saints and interacted with them. I have interviewed many of them, and the interviews make up a number of my books.

I do not endorse people seeking visits and encounters with saints, and I personally believe that every encounter needs to be initiated and managed by the Holy Spirit. But I am fully supportive of people interacting with the great cloud of witnesses as mentioned in Hebrews 12:1.

Angels

It is my belief that each person, both the saved and unsaved, have a personal guardian angel. I believe that it is possible for a Christian to find out their angel's name and interact with them.

I know that each angel has permission from God regarding what they can do and say. Some angels are not allowed to speak with you, and no coaxing by you will change their minds as they would be disobeying their orders.

It is totally credible for a person in ministry to have multiple angels, each with assigned duties to fulfill in their life. I have several angels: a scribe angel, Bethany; a prophetic angel, Michael, who is also my guardian angel; and a finance angel, Mark, who makes sure that I always have the funds I need to publish books. I have an angel that is the head of all my angels named Elisha. I personally believe that the stronger and bigger your anointing, the more angels that are assigned to you. I believe that people like Joyce Meyer and Benny Hinn have thousands of angels attached to their ministry.

Many people are excited about angels. Some of these people do not have an intimate relationship with Jesus. Jesus knows how to make sure people have a safe and secure relationship with him before these people start to interact regularly with angels.

Commanding Angels
A number of people I admire say that there is no scriptural evidence for a saint to be able to command angels, so they preach against it. All I can say is that I have often had thousands of angels turn up for me, and, when I asked the Holy Spirit about it, I was told to dispatch them. I sought the Lord for a viable mission for them, gave them orders, and saw them go. I tend to give long missions that will take a lot of time.

From time to time, thousands of angels come back, and I dispatch them again, and they go. I do not know of any scripture references for this apart from Jesus saying that he could have prevented his death by dispatching legions of angels. (See Matthew 26:53.)

Like anything, people can operate in excess in this area, and some seem misguided in this, but I don't personally speak out unless I am asked to by the Holy Spirit.

I have always had a good relationship with angels and don't in any way see myself as superior to them. See my books, *My Radical Encounters with Angels: Book 1* and *My Radical Encounters with Angels: Book 2*, for more of my experiences.

The Holy Spirit
The Holy Spirit personally directs and guides me, and I could not live an effective Christian life without his indwelling presence to empower me.

The Holy Spirit further manifests himself through numerous gifts, which are still valid today. Each believer possesses at least one gift and often more to minister to believers and unbelievers alike in power and in love. While the five-fold ministry—the offices of apostle, prophet, pastor, teacher, and evangelist—is integral to the building up of the Body of Christ, these are not the only gifts present in the Body today. Additional gifts include the working of miracles, healing, helping others, administration, unknown tongues, interpretation of tongues, exhortation, giving, and mercy. Each believer can walk in greater fullness and effectiveness of his or her calling when they are operating in the gifts as designed by God.

My Calling
I found out twelve years ago that I was called to be a prophet. I have given about twenty thousand prophecies so far, and through books and Facebook groups, I have mentored many people called to the prophetic office. I personally believe that you need to be called to ministry and that God will only give you his favor when you have been called.

Today, I spend most of my time writing books as a teacher of the Word. I consider it a great honor and privilege to teach the people of God and to write evangelistic books for unbelievers. I thank the Lord that he continually supplies me with finances to self-publish books that he puts on my heart to write.

Today, with Facebook and YouTube, anyone can teach. But not all of the people that teach have a calling from God to teach. I respect everyone who does their best to follow their heart's desires, though.

A few years ago, Jesus gave me a vision and told me that I would write fifty books. Recently the Father increased that number and told me that I would write as many as ninety books or more. My calling is to write as many as God inspires me to write. You can support me in this mission by being my friend on Facebook, praying for me, or donating to me.

False Prophets

The Old Testament says that a false prophet is someone that leads you to worship another God. If you read more than five of my books, you will see that a constant theme of mine is that people should leave behind the ways of the world, follow Jesus, and obey what Jesus taught in his commands.

A false prophet could lead you to follow them, and sadly some do. A false prophet might operate in a spirit that is not of the Lord.

Any person who has read my posts on Facebook and who knows of my writings, both interviews with saints and others, will see that Jesus is my Lord, my Savior, my source, and my inspiration.

I'd love to hear from you

One of the ways that you can bless me as a writer is by writing an honest and candid review of my book on Amazon. I always read the reviews of my books, and I would love to hear what you have to say about this one.

Before I buy a book, I read the reviews first. You can make an informed decision about a book when you have read enough honest reviews from readers. One way to help me sell this book and to give me positive feedback is by writing a review for me. It doesn't cost you a thing but helps me and the future readers of this book enormously.

To read my blog, request a life-coaching session, request your own personal prophecy, request a visit to heaven, or to receive a personal message from your angel, you can also visit my website at http://personal-prophecy-today.com as linked. All of the funds raised through my ministry website will go toward the books that I write and self-publish.

You can also request a trip to heaven with Robin Gann. You can find her contact information on my website.

To write to me about this book or to share any other thoughts, please feel free to contact me at survivors.sanctuary@gmail.com which is my personal email address.

You can also friend request me on Facebook at Matthew Robert Payne. Please send me a message if we have no friends in common as a lot of scammers now send me friend requests.

You can also do me a huge favor and share this book on Facebook as a recommended book to read. This will help me and other readers.

If you have any editing needs, you can contact my editor, Lisa Thompson, at writebylisa@gmail.com for assistance.

How to Sponsor a Book Project

If you have been blessed by this book, you might consider sponsoring a book for me. It normally costs me between $1,500 and $2,000 or more to produce each book that I write, depending on the length of the book.

If you seek the Holy Spirit about financing a book for me, I know that the Lord would be eternally grateful to you. Consider how much this book has blessed you and then think of hundreds or even thousands of people who would be blessed by a book of mine. As you are probably aware, the vast majority of my books are ninety-nine cents on Kindle, which proves to you that book writing is indeed a ministry for me and not a money-making venture. I would be very happy if you supported me in this.

If you have any questions for me, or if you want to know what projects I am currently working on that your money might finance, you can write to me at survivors.sanctuary@gmail.com and ask me for more information. I would be pleased to give you more details about my projects.

You can sow any amount to my ministry by simply sending me money via the PayPal link at this address: http://personal-prophecy-today.com/support-my-ministry/ You can be sure that your support, no matter the amount, will be used for the publishing of helpful Christian books for people to read.

Other Books by Matthew Robert Payne

The Prophetic Supernatural Experience

Prophetic Evangelism Made Simple

Your Identity in Christ

His Redeeming Love: A Memoir

Writing and Self-Publishing Christian Nonfiction

Coping with your Pain and Suffering

Living for Eternity

Jesus Speaking Today

Great Cloud of Witnesses Speak

My Radical Encounters with Angels

Finding Intimacy with Jesus Made Simple

My Radical Encounters with Angels: Book 2

A Beginner's Guide to the Prophetic

Michael Jackson Speaks from Heaven

7 Keys to Intimacy with Jesus

Conversations with God: Book 1

Optimistic Visions of Revelation

Conversations with God: Book 2

Finding Your Purpose in Christ

Influencing your World for Christ: Practical Everyday
Evangelism

Deep Calls unto Deep: Answering Questions on the
Prophetic

My Visits to the Galactic Council of Heaven

The Parables of Jesus Made Simple: Updated and
Expanded Edition

Great Cloud of Witnesses Speak: Old and New

Walking under an Open Heaven

A Message from My Angel: Book 1

Interviews with the Two Witnesses: Enoch and Elijah
Speak

Gaining Freedom from Sex Addictions: Breaking Free of
Pornography and Prostitutes

Mary Magdalene Speaks from Heaven: A Divine Revelation

Princess Diana Speaks from Heaven: A Divine Revelation

How to Hear God's Voice: Keys to Conversational Two-Way Prayer

Apostle John Speaks from Heaven: A Divine Revelation

You can find my published books on my Amazon author page here: http://tinyurl.com/jq3h893

Upcoming Books

Christian Discipleship Made Simple

Apostle Peter Speaks from Heaven: A Divine Revelation

About Matthew Robert Payne

Matthew was raised in a Baptist church and was led to the Lord at the tender age of eight. He has experienced some pain and darkness in his life, which has given him a deep compassion and love for all people.

Today, he's an administrator in a Facebook group called "Prophetic Training Platform," and he invites you to join him there. Matthew has a commission from the Lord to train up prophets and to mentor others in the Christian faith. He does this through his Facebook posts and by writing relevant books on the Christian faith.

God has commissioned him to write at least fifty books in his life, and he spends his days writing and earning the money to self-publish. You can support him by donating money at http://personal-prophecy-today.com or by requesting any of his other services available through his ministry website.

It is Matthew's prayer that this book has blessed you, and he hopes it will lead you into a deeper and more intimate relationship with God.